Gallery Books

Editor Peter Fallon

IN A TOWN OF FIVE THOUSAND PEOPLE

Frank McGuinness

IN A TOWN OF
FIVE THOUSAND
PEOPLE

Gallery Books

In A Town of Five Thousand People
is first published
simultaneously in paperback
and in a clothbound edition
on 30 October 2012.

The Gallery Press
Loughcrew
Oldcastle
County Meath
Ireland

www.gallerypress.com

ISBN 978 1 85235 545 6 *paperback*
     978 1 85235 546 3 *clothbound*

A CIP catalogue record for this book
is available from the British Library.

Contents

for John and Kate Doherty

How to Build Your Gondola

after Canaletto's 'Rio del Medicanti'

for Brian Friel

Don't beggar yourself settling in Venice.
Avoid glitzy squares and bejewelled bridges
leading to more glitzy squares that connect
bejewelled bridges with mansions hewn from air.
The doge and all his courtiers, scheming,
scholarly, dressed in furs of their wildest dreams,
flaunting all they have — it is all they have —
when they pass, ignore them, they'll be removed.
Bear in mind you've come to Venice to learn
how to build your gondola — a working craft,
a vessel, to ferry ancestral milk
and furniture, bed linen, bits of time
they scavenged and tied to their humpy backs
when they charged the Grand Canal and rested,
turning up their noses at Torcello's spuds,
refusing to dine on food fit for tinkers.
Their like provides wood for your gondola
fashioned into clothes lines of shirts and socks,
togs and trousers, rags of your livery.
You've served your time, you've survived in Venice.

PART ONE

The Town Next To Us

Never liked it much — the town next to us.
They had the works — ambulance, hospitals.
Not even their signposts showed where we live.
Their bosses were model, their bakeries gold
as wheat plundered from our ovens to feed
the all, the sundry of Inishowen,
Tyrconnell, every art and every part
of godforsaken, glorious Donegal.

The people right plasters of Paris,
the streets long white streaks of gypsum,
take the eye from your head, bite from your mouth,
tyres and wheels under your vehicle.
There were twenty-three hours in our day —
those bastards had stolen a march on us.
They thrived on big feeds and mountains of wine;
never put their hands into their pockets.

It's said the same hands were strangers to water.
Soap was rare as a word of welcome.
It snowed at Easter — their Christmas was shite.
The heat of summer brought them out in hives.
Too mean to scratch their scaly hides, they scrimped —
they saved a fortune hoarding dirty cans
of beans and peas to feed their families.
Bad weed grows well; they thrived in poisoned fields.

They rented out the holy church to Moonies
and to Hare Krishnas — could they have luck
dancing nude before the tabernacle,
speaking in tongues as false as their teeth?
Any wonder their sons and strange daughters
defied their mad marriage beds, divorcing
in Satanic worship of the four winds
that blew their breed ashore to the next town.

They cut the throats of innocent women.
They drank their blood from skulls of virgins.
They kept as pets a pack of wolves — no child
was saved from their temptation of fancy
biscuits — Jaffa Cakes, USA Assortment,
Kimberley, Mikado, Coconut Creams —
Jacobs and Japs, South African miners —
I swear to Christ that kip was jammed with them.

It had to come to a very bad end.
It did when lightning struck twenty-three times.
Who can explain the sympathy of fire?
It took a scundering to the town next to us.
Its flames did clothe their naked shamelessness.
We heard them weeping in alien words.
Ambulance, hospitals did not save them.
There being no signposts, what could we do?

Portrait of Myself with My Imaginary Wife

Mother died of starvation.
In the photograph we sent Father,
taken in orange, taken in grey,
dressed entirely in pink, dressed in white,
her veil her face, her face two lips,
lips do not move, they do not eat,
saying the colour grey, the colour orange.
In the photograph we sent Father
she bandaged her famished hands
and fed them to the son who survived her.
Did he?
Every woman I meet now I marry,
saying, let me feed you,
let me be your mother.

The Fox Fight

in memory of Eileen McDaid

At five in the morning
I heard the fox
who settled in my garden
have a fight to the death
with her own shadow,
her wails an iron cross
she'd feed to her cubs
instead of her blood.

I carry in my shoe
the clay of my garden,
my feet two hungry cubs
devouring my belly,
wailing through my veins,
looking for their mother,
looking for her blood,
at five in the morning.

I felt the same blood
run through my veins
as I stood alone
at my aunt's grave
lamenting her first and last,
the weight of her coffin
dislocating
my shoulder blades.

May I take as my tribe
the starving vixen's belly
dining on clay,
gargling on grief,

in battle with our shadows,
my weapon an iron cross
dislocating
my shoulder blades.

Francis Bacon

I had an ancestor who invented the fridge.
He died of cold, proving his thesis.
I'd like what I paint to freeze like hell
and squeal like those popes Jesus punished
for wearing frocks and pretending to be men.
I see life through the green delicious lens
of champagne bottles I down with pleasure.

If I had a sister I'd call her Cassandra.
I'd marry her, were she the marrying kind.
Let her prophesy our incestuous doom.
Were we to have a child it would be red
and Roman Catholic, and it would be ugly,
this ridiculous child, so I'd sacrifice it.
Would it be son or daughter? Neither, neither.

I'd request an audience with my father,
to ask advice what it is to be father.
He would produce a whip, a horse, a belt,
and I'd feel my father's cock as belt,
as horse, as whip; my blood would be paint
on my obedient flesh, a strange tattoo,
a mark of Cain when Father proposed marriage.

Parents are strange — they remember their children.
I remember my mother as if she were the child,
the child bleeding from her father's whip.
She cries as her husband sets his curs on her.
They leap and lick her with affection.
That is what men do to their women, leap, lick —
the greyhound teeth of their tenderness.

Painting should kill like an innocent animal;
painting should be like my mother's clothes.
We fit — two hands tattooed blue and red.

I scent my face with almond champagne.
I smell my lovers on the stains of my fingers.
I crucify those men; they crucify my father.
How long it lasts, this *marriage blanc*.

Furniture of Eileen Gray

Count me among the fallen.
The story of my sins
may be contained in wood.
I opened my brown boots
and smelt the stains of linseed.
My eyes shed seven tears,
see if you can count them.
Blowing my stash of doubloons,
I shared my mug of arrach.
I squashed the fruit of Asia,
dousing the Pyrenees.
I planted in its forests
what it is I seem to be —
the story of my sins,
a furniture of gallows.

Morehampton Road

I defend myself on Morehampton Road
from ghosts and griefs, from inexplicable
sorrows that take their toll. My sofa bed
too short for my body, a Book of Kells
contorted letter painted blue on black,
sleepless, that's where I slept, glad of shelter —
the girls enduring the sweat of my shoes
souring the flat with their rancid leather.
Herbert Park, the tennis courts, the railings.
Refuge I fled to when breakfast erupted —
forks in the ceiling, spoons in the ceiling.
Live and let live, or you're out on your tod.
Joining the dole queues, feeding hand to mouth,
you walk the streets of seventies Dublin,
the city's manners neither graceful nor couth —
stop to your gallop and clip to your wings.
Back in Donnybrook it's changed times indeed —
meeting bank managers giving advice
why I should decamp to where profits lead,
following fashion, losing a fortune.
I order a decaf in McCloskey's.
Down in one go, no sugar to sweeten
the ghosts, the griefs, inexplicable wherefores,
trillions of reasons to love the heathen —
seductive the kiss between man and man.
X marks the spot where I learned secret codes,
sweet as Sunday missing every Mass.
I defend myself on Morehampton Road.

Shoes

after Michelangelo

If I were to flay
the skin of my back
and turn it into shoes
for you to wear —

what would you do
with my sacrifice
of neck and fin,
of spine and arse?

Would you watch me
fall,
a horse
from the heavens,
play football with my soul,
kick my bones skywards?

The Latin Mass

I clerked the last Latin Mass
in St Mary's Oratory,
or was supposed to, but slept in.
Heady days after Vatican Two —
we would all be as one
worshipping Christ in our lingo,
and the Prods — the blessèd enemy —
would come to love the Virgin,
so we'd forgive their trespass.
Likely as moon transplanting sun.
Faith of our fathers survived.

Durham

Is theos burch breome geond Breotenrice

for Alan Donnelly

The servants of the Lord live in Durham.
They wait for the river to cease flowing.
For the birds to abandon the dense forest.
For the wild beasts to drown with the great fish
that feed on the preserved, most venerated
bones of beautiful Aidan and chaste Bede —
their tombs hard as the heart of the good Lord,
who built this city, renowned throughout Britain,
from the rock that shed martyr's blood, the head
that fell from the shoulders of King Oswald.
He worked his miracles and tamed the birds,
the beasts, the river, the rock, the creation
of earth, the stars, the sun and moon in Durham.
The fish are a different kettle of faith.

The Erasmus House

I hatched the egg Erasmus laid.
                              — *Martin Luther*

1

Anderlecht is packed each Saturday.
We passed through the market of meat and cheese,
flowers in splendid vases, sweets to die for,
cheap clothes taken from the respectable backs
of people pawning them to finance their habit
of books. Better to starve than want learning.
The herbs in this garden remedy pangs
from childbirth and fever — miraculous
cures can be found in purple sage and fennel,
thriving transplanted in the library
of rain and of rock and of sweat from your brow —
hard labour Erasmus avoided.

2

Lent is the season for martyrs and eggs.
Break your fast on the hard bread and water
left out to soften and warm in the air
the sweet winds of spring take the chill from.
So you might think, but we are in Belgium.
February is a carnivore month.
Hoovers are cleaning the Erasmus House.
People who work there are concerned the din
will give the wrong impression to tourists
praying for the soul of just who they like
to canonize. There is dust everywhere,
for unto dust we as pilgrims do return.

3

The music of lutes has left these four walls.
The icon himself stares from each cranny,
angry at noise of machine and mankind.
He wants peace, he wants quiet — play outside.
Do not disturb the father and mother
of Europe before the atomic breach
no herbs from the garden can remedy.
Neat grass is parched orange in summertime.
Heatwaves can scorch the streets of Anderlecht.
We can flock then to the Erasmus House.
Bury the hatchet in the martyr's back.
Break open eggs — picnic on the passion.

Berlin

in memory of Bunty Pike 1915-2008

If I must perish, please — not in Berlin,
sipping Russian wine, feasting on lion,
among the ladies of the Tiergarten,
starved of menfolk through the war's long ration.
I shared a flat with Unity Mitford,
her hat like something out of Noah's Ark
hungry citizens boiled up for their feed
of poisoned phoenix and lashings of pork.
The Lindenstrasse reminds me of home,
were home a place to visit and vanish.
I had three children to walk hand in hand
round the zoo and fountain, making a wish.
I abandoned Berlin for apron strings,
the fall of reichs, the fear of perishing.

The Pergamon Museum

for David and Carola Lewis

Lions of Babylon guard you.
Fields of Assyria feed you,
and let Dionysus dance
attendance on your marriage bed.
The maenads prepare wedding meats.
The satyr gives birth to itself.
The mask is the madness of love.
The gods have returned to your lives.

The Flowers of the Forest

Was he the life and soul of the party,
acting the idiot at closing time?

Were they laughing like drains, his best mates,
bidding him farewell and see you later?

Did he look for Chinese or Indian,
a last fish supper for the condemned man?

Did he reach for his mobile phone to murmur
sweet nothings, his last will and testament?

Was he found without shirt, without trousers,
his bones on his sleeve, his heart stripped bare?

Did he cry for his wife and his children,
did nightingales bleed from his forehead?

Did he darken the door — did banshees wail —
did he dance in the street where his face fell?

Did his garden grow with his father's tears?
Did they play the flowers of the forest?

The Abbey Players

I MARIE KEAN

When Stanley Kubrick lit me
as Barry Lyndon's mother
it was like Raphael's 'Madonna'
bidding farewell to her son,
seeing him for the first time
leaving her for eternity,
looking into brazen candlelight —
one million Annunications.

I could be angel or demon
depending on my humour —
forgetful, melancholic,
inclined to let the moment
of what it was possessed me
to do what in the first place
it was I decided to do,
come hell or come high water.

I had no more intention
of drowning in compliments
than the man in the holy moon
of descending on this globe,
here where he'd be ill at ease
far from his lunar creatures,
leaving footprints in the dust,
like myself on the Abbey stage.

2 DONAL McCANN

I resist the pull — the twist — the turn
of what I know not to be right. I shade each
word, each phrase, with light only I can see.

The elephant in the living room,
the walrus docked itself in the garden,
that's what I work best with — carving delicate
bark and bite from the roughest ivory.
Marie Kean knits — drives me to distraction.
I lay at her feet the fruits of my big game.
My healing hands caress beasts back to life.

3 FEDELMA CULLEN

For once in my life I am too early.
This death is for the birds — shocking exit.
The same flesh of birds, they chant in chorus
some kind of Greek tragedy: man is born
and grows into a thing of wonder, fades —
like dew upon the rose, withers into —

for the love of Jesus, enough weeping!
All my days I have believed in courage.
I lived with Daniel in our lion's den.
We tamed the bees and dined on wild honey.
The smile on my face was sweet as his kiss.
We wrote the book when it came to goodbyes.

4 JOAN O'HARA

I am a woman who hails from the west.
Heaven would be my idea of hell.
I can see multitudes in pitch darkness.
Sweet as blackberries, rancid as hazel.

The bogeyman cometh, giving no quarter.
That's how I'd measure out wee sweetie balls.

I douse my bare pelt in Seapoint water.
It brings me to life like a holy well.

Taking a flight on my sturdiest wings,
I landed not a million miles from home.
Sligo equipped me with arrows and slings.
I stand as I stand, its flesh on my bones.

5 RAY McANALLY

One day in Donegal — my heart crosswise —
didn't a blackbird out of the blue
sing the entire score of *Madam Butterfly* —
Nagasaki turned into Buncrana,
the town of my birth, but my father moved,
being a bankman subject to the whims,
the moods of where head office would send him —
much like myself, a travelling player
in the chancy business of art, money,
managing companies on the breadline,
dreaming of jam and hearing strange blackbirds
breaking their hearts at being abandoned.

A whispered aside can deafen a house,
if the whisperer knows what he's doing —
a ghost in the making, haunting the air,
confessing sins of the flesh and the mind
to a heavenly father, a mother
past caring, all their fingers worn to the bone,
creating a garden children play in,
fall, cut themselves, get up and recover,
swinging like bats upside down by the wings
they'll use to go hunting, gathering prey

as their fancy may take them — look, a toad
or rat — if they have luck, a blackbird.

Right down the gullet in one mighty go,
a drouth on them fit for a Moville man
who swam Lough Foyle and crossed back again —
hungry Leander smelling soda bread,
dying for a feed of bacon and eggs
cracked in a bowl of magnificent hue —
the sun at Aileach its correspondence,
there where three counties of Ulster are seen,
and playing King Lear one town to the next
I was monarch of that ravishing realm
begging the gods not to let me be mad —
for once in their life the blighters listened.

There is no secret about great acting,
no mystery but breath and butterfly —
it's easier than working down a mine
digging for coal or some precious metal
a blackbird carries buried in its throat
and scatters through air, riotous, spendthrift,
sharing the gold of Donegal mornings
where I set forth to conquer the new world
speaking no Spanish but well versed in lore
that opened the earth if chanted in time —
I tune with that most mysterious
secret — which would be telling, so I'll stop.

The Cavendish Lab

for Alma and James Cullen

I saw Kafka in the Cavendish Lab
trying to perfect his command of Czech,
his face a mask of chromosomes X, Y,
dreaming of Prague, generations that pass,
lined up like specimens, bottles of ash,
there to be cherished till the cows come home,
churning their butter back into sour milk,
horns sharp as talons, wild as the eagle —
the eagle that carries Ganymede back
to the arms of apostle Abraham,
sacrificing the golden calf of his son,
begetting his name, calling him Kafka,
trying to perfect his command of Czech,
dreaming of Prague in the Cavendish Lab.

Roland Barthes

The ways of Eros are manifold;
the whys of Eros are manifold.

Definite articles astonish:
I do not suffer from lack of them.

Like Catholics, death is everywhere;
a pain in the pleasure of the arse.

I paid Charon with coins of the realm
minted from gold in my lover's teeth.

Waiting and watching where the roads cross,
we ask for alms from a tsaddik.

He answers our prayers with silence;
he'd take the hand from you with hunger.

A holy man begs for rainwater —
the sky wears a strange Japanese mask.

My mother weaves a veil of red milk;
I'd stake my life on her cleanliness.

The ways of Eros are manifold;
the whys of Eros are manifold.

Walter Benjamin

I give my address
as the moons of Jupiter.
That's where you'll find
all that belong to me.
Who asks what I've done for
the moons of Jupiter?
Tell them I bequeathed
my body to that planet.

What motion is it
guides the moons of Jupiter?
The kingdom, the power,
the glory of my grief.
You can see my bones
on the moons of Jupiter.
Pray to them while
you commit my sins.

Dressed in robes woven from
the moons of Jupiter,
I am as lonely as
Galileo Galilei,
contemplating the cosmos
on the moons of Jupiter
as he collects the fauna
and flora of the galaxy.

I am crowned Emperor
of the moons of Jupiter,
tonight as I take
the universe in my hand.
I send them all spinning,
the moons of Jupiter,
into the chaos,
the mayhem of light.

Jacques Derrida

Encasing my hand
in a crystal glove,
finger by finger
I crack the glass,
serving champagne
in flutes of shard,
milky as marble,
soft as firing squads,
quenching the bloodlust
of dry multitudes
standing on stairways
forgetting their lines.

Mouths full of plum,
teeth in a brace,
words are weapons
of pandemonium.
Talk of the devil
beside the angels.
See the darkness
within the darkness.

The Child of Prague

for Claire Keegan

A woman once married a widowed man —
that's where I'd look to this story starting.
She sat in her kitchen, deaf to the world,
and could hear her heart beating up her throat,
spilling out sounds like blood circulating,
washing the floors and staining the windows,
smashing the glass she hands to her husband
who lies beside the lassie neglected.
Breathing her last as if they were courting,
her widowed man and a girl growing deaf
to warnings, prayers, her crying parents —
she'll do whatever he asks her to do.

He'll take her heart and boil it to bury
the hatchet of their life as man and wife,
pledging their troth before the Child of Prague
you leave on your sill come the wedding day,
for good weather, good fortune and God bless.
It's the like of him would know how to sing
'I'll take you home again, Kathleen' — but where?
A room where bride and maid, one and the same,
are the wife he thrice did the dirty on —
a ghost who should know better but doesn't.
For luck she leaves the Child of Prague headless.
Neither now hear her saying bad words.

Cigarettes

Before they died
within ten months
of each other, like
starving children, my
mother, father
in hospital
beds, hospital
wards, they both begged
for cigarettes,
a box of matches,
and I forked out.
When was it I
myself gave up?
Four — five — years on.

PART TWO

The Book of Hours

1 HAIR

How many colours in one woman's hair?
It is red as badness, grey as silence.
The comb is steel in the cold water jug.
The comb, the water, the jug are sisters.
One is sitting, one stands in silence.
The silence is speaking the name 'sister'.
How many colours in the comb and jug?
There is red water in one woman's hair.

2 ORSINO

I cannot forget the name of that horse —
Orsino that won the Cesarewitch.
I cannot forget the odds it came in —
the precise amount of October cash.
I cannot forget I did not win it —
first past the post but then disqualified.
I cannot forget the surfeit of shock —
the soles of my shoes were letting in rain.

3 ROAD

The shirt factory gates closed at two sharp —
a strict hour after eating your dinner,
your grub padlocked to the chain of your gut.
A widow woman asked me to fashion
a blouse for her daughter's First Communion
from scraps of discarded white coloured cloth.
I did the decent thing. They found me out.
They showed me the road: I walked with head high.

4 LEMON'S SWEETS

There is a chance I will eat Lemon's Sweets
before the Easter when Christmas is gone.
He will hand me forgotten sugar's stain
to kiss my teeth like remembered regret.
I will bury my heart in the hard box
that spells out the sweet and the sour desire,
smelling white nougat and blazing cherry.
I remember and regret Lemon's Sweets.

5 GLENS

A big night once in my crowded kitchen —
I should construct the green glens of Antrim.
I sang out my heart at the strange request
with visions of Babylon — a garden
for you, a garden for me, the garden
where the Euphrates and Crana
cradled my children between rivers, safe
and sound in my arms, far from green glens.

6 RICE

The rice that is cooking in my oven —
it could feed all the millions of China,
a miracle of fish, and Asia.
Rice that smelled of hunger and strawberries,
plagued the din of locust and cockroach
devouring the black, the burning of rice,
as Irish as welcome to my parlour,
burning, breaking green bread in sodden fields.

7 HAWK

I'm like a hawk surveying my garden.
The cats still enter — the black and white beasts.
They come back like ghosts to feed me with dreams.
My dreams of greyhounds, kept in the old forge —
I smell the dogs' chains in my father's eyes.
The hawks tore the throats of black and white cats.
Pursued by her dreams, fleeing from the chains,
who was the hawk flying into freedom?

8 PLUMS

The boys dressed in purple fed on diamonds —
diamonds large as plums, hard as plum stones.
The blood in their veins was sweet as the juice
that trickled like sweat — it may have been sweat —
from the limbs of the self-same purple boys
whose arms caressed their bejewelled bodies
narrow and white as hyacinth blossoms
speaking of cold, of crazed, ravenous boys.

9 MAZE

My sister's husband went on his rampage —
a minotaur in the bed of their maze,
drinking himself mad on rotten poitín,
distilled from heathers of volcanic Crete.
Bag and baggage, that's where we halted, feet
bleeding from the shoes for our wedding toes,
cramped between bells and silver rings, his nose
the breath he slipped inside her, naked-red.

10 SISTERS

Our hair a riot of love and sisters,
we can cackle till our heart's discontent,
as if we'd shave each other clean as pins
washed in the blood of the riotous lamb,
its wool, the soft, the luxuriant rope
binding my hands, my hair to the great gas —
talking secrets in the cackling darkness,
my heart her head, my sister to silence.

11 THE LOST SON

I receive a letter from my lost son.
Mother, I manage in this, my exile.
I believe we pass through this galaxy —
our town and its buildings' geography
alleyways to stars, their mound of secrets.
I study with patience and with passion
my life's most riotous constellations.
Mother, I miss you, in this, my exile.

12 BONES

A yellow dog defied all reasoning.
How could it be the colour of saffron?
It fed on scraps from the kitchen table,
the cloth bearing witness to the rainbow
lining the coats, lining the pockets, full
to the brim with manna from heaven, soft
quail's flesh roasting in hell, a yellow dog
choking and gasping for enormous bones.

13 VEINS

My sons, my daughters, all those never born —
I trace the map of their lives in my veins.
You would be amazed at the direction,
at the way I've been, I am, I will be —
at how the blood of my being is blood
from the man I loved who left me no child.
I trace the map of his life in my veins,
my sons, my daughters, all those never born.

14 SOUP

What point in spilling beans or crying wolf?
Who could milk soup out of bricks and mortar,
season the house with sorrow's condiments?
Let it grow cold, untasted, well hidden.
Why pour out truth into a begging bowl,
a bridge broken, a cracked willow pattern?
No man nor woman, neither friend nor foe,
in their right or wrong mind would drink such soup.

15 STEW

I threw out that soup — it tasted of blood.
I'll dish up a stew of earthy flowers,
the clay attached to their magical roots,
Aurorean source of forgetfulness.
What will happen to those who eat this spell?
They will be filled with breathtaking almonds,
a crimson meat of poisonous tongue, soft
as purple wine, turning to vinegar.

16 UNICORN

I would like to tell a shocking story.
I tamed and rode upon a unicorn.
Imagine its surprise to feel my boot
or clog, my bare or my two stockinged feet,
in full command of this mystical beast.
The bastard then hurled me arse over heel
from the broken sky into Buncrana
where I lost the run of my unicorn.

17 FORGE

I got a glimpse of myself in a knife,
a fork, a spoon — the box of cutlery.
It took a shine to me breathing my last
near death's gateway, entering the forge — forge
my first, my glimpse of myself, the knife, fork
eating fish and chips in Derry City,
laying siege to Roaring Meg's minions.
What fire could smelt the iron of myself?

18 THE BACK YARD

Anything can happen in the back yard.
No house nor garden fronts on your freedom.
You climb a wall into something stranger.
You don't know what is going to happen.
I'd say the best you'd hope for — very best —
I'd say pray hard enough — you might, just might —
perhaps you'll get it — you could be lucky.
I never climbed the wall. I trusted none.

19 THE GIRLS SCHOOL

The girls school terrified the rich and poor.
Like Satan, one nun had her special ways.
She held us down to black and blue our minds.
My sister bore marks of those blood beatings.
Fuckers, they got away with sheer murder.
We'd let them do whatever would please them.
I wonder what part of hell they burn in.
I'd feed that fire with their sally rods.

20 DREAMS

Nights that I cannot sleep I can still dream —
dreams that come to me in all shade and shapes.
Far from the isolation ward of time
I come out to play, and it lifts my heart.
A child again, going to the girls school,
I'm taught to read, to write, to tell what hour,
in what location dwells the alpine flower.
I am yellow, white — a dream of still sleep.

21 FIRE

Water can put out the warmest, loudest fire.
The red dies when the silver bites the dust,
and sweepers clean the gold out from water.
It is said they make an absolute fortune.
I'd say they survive on the smoke of fags,
the glorious twelfth of never say die,
an Orange march the smell of sweet petrol.
I peel the rind of water and fire.

22 SCOTLAND

America — never wanted to go.
Nobody ever asked me to make that leap —
throw a leg across the Atlantic Ocean.
Scotland, that was more than sufficient.
I saw the Gorbals. They were the Gorbals.
Aunt Mary working — a Trojan working
to keep the tenements Augean clean.
Glasgow — Gorbals — never wanted to go.

23 EGGS

I cannot eat eggs any shape or form.
They turn my stomach, be it with child,
be it without the egg that breaks into birth.
I've smelt their taste in the cleanest kitchens
where spiders webbed the best of crockery
locked up in country people's dressers,
for fear the men's rough hands might break them
into the yolk, the white of eggs turning my stomach.

24 WATER

The earth has stopped, and my sister has died.
I see her face in the bony coffin.
She's the one put pins into my red hair.
Older than she, younger than my parents,
I am sister to moon, daughter to ocean.
Love is my nature, and I've paid the price.
I make a dinner for my family.
Carrots, potatoes, stewing steak, water.

PART THREE

Heligan

God does not like Cornwall. He placed it in England,
far from Equatorial Guinea, the Hesperides,
the Amazonian Basin, deepest recess of the Indies,
a score of locations where it would be happier.
This is what the wisteria whispers in its madness,
deciphering the Rorschach blots of flowers that bloom
when the mood and meaning take them, fully intending
to marry well with the most fertile vegetation,
the red skies, the family of voracious barn owls
that plunder the seven seas of Heligan's gardens.

The gardens make themselves ill from a strict diet
of stone and water blurring the features and structure
of their bones like Nottingham alabasters
knocked about a bit by soldiers in search of gold statues,
wanting their pay, feeding on insects, breaking
the sun dial in the mirrored greenness — land time forgot.
It has taken decades for the bracken and blisters,
the thorn of the dog rose, the alligator teethmarks
left on the welcome mat for ten thousand visitors,
to do damage we must seek to remedy.

And remedy is found in pits of exotic fruits,
the melon, the pineapple, watered like Mesopotamia,
these pits where famished architects of peace and plenty
once toiled to feed the refined, the pale appetites
that came to Heligan and clogged up their softness
to the cries of the damned, the sweat of tin mines,
Jacob's ladder rising from the bowels of the earth
putting flesh of their feet on the narrow rungs of clay
God breathed into life when he created Cornwall,
transporting it far from its native jungle soil.

There is a jungle still in its mesh of kith and kin
rearing their young in the verdant tenements of light.

Male swallows fuck and leg it from the nest —
who is going to follow them all the way to Egypt?
Heligan is watching their crime and punishment
and plots its clean revenge in the snares and shocks
of the sun's barb wire fence which tears the feathered wing,
bleeds the broken egg, takes the dying cells
and flings them in the air like a crazed juggler
entertaining the crowd with hit and miss accuracy.

Accurate is the heart that hears the beating of Heligan,
defying the hand of God destroying time's beauty,
laying waste the pathways, the trellis, the house itself,
as if the human body were sufficient law to heal
whatever is brought low or broken or blighted.
Heligan believes in the blood's resurrection.
It rises from the hospital bed and spits on bad luck.
It is one with the red sky, the absconding swallow,
the melon pit, the tin mines, the mirrored sun dial.
It's come back from the war, a miracle, a soldier.

Rooms in Denmark

after Hammershøi

1

A priest from Copenhagen blessed the sun.
He dreamt in a forest of silver birch.
A hawk broke the windows of his grey house,
giving him visions of rooms in Denmark.

2

And grey grows the lilac, the lavender too,
the mountain of lilies — balm to my eyes —
in the gardens besieging Brunswick Square
changed if you will to Odense and Aarhus.

3

What power moves the doors opening themselves
to white tabernacles of divine chairs
and tables costing a fortune to buy
for the house, Number 30, Strandgate?

4

The smell of bacon pervades this blessing —
pigs in the parlour and mud in your eye —
but Circe's magic cannot harm the men
who come as pilgrims to rooms in Denmark.

5

The darkening sky is pure Lutheran,
its shadows are sin, a blasphemous child —
empty is empty as hammer and tongs
snatch fire from angels, rejecting Satan.

6

A girl turns her back, asking for silence,
and silence she got to her heart's content,
stitching the secrets of her life in threads
woven from snow in Antarctica's fields.

7

I carved from ice the priest and his blessing;
I made chairs and doors from tabernacles;
I caught in a cage a lavender hawk.
Its song was visions of rooms in Denmark.

The Health of the Sea

for Isabelle Famchon

All that summer was the coast of Japan.
A man who came from purest mermaid stock,
my father took my face in his rough voice.
We will not drown like rats in a barrel.
My daughter, eat and drink this feast of brine.
I did not relish the wind's salt and pepper,
the rice of waves in my pudding bowl hair.
Then I saw Father bless the Pacific.
A lawyer well versed in shifts of passion,
he absolved the water of my murder.
He produced a bottle of kosher wine
though we observed no dietary laws.
We drank a toast to the health of the sea.
It was weaker than Father — we survived.

Aleppo

The white boys of Aleppo
gathered to play tennis
in the copper mines of Syria.
Their court became a souk,
a citadel, a monument
to fairness and trade.
Their hair was young,
in a tangle of sweat,
their limbs like marble milk
while they observed
the rules, the procedures,
the proper scores
as scores were settled
by their luck and skill.

They had travelled to Aleppo
for reasons most chose
to keep entirely to themselves,
being connoisseurs
of secrets, of signs
it was no one's business
to divulge in such a manner
that might harm the men
who sent them on assignment
to play by
the rules, the procedures,
the proper scores
as scores were settled
by their luck and skill.

In the heat of Aleppo
they desired the cold drink
of each other's copper sweat
running down their necks
salty as the sand,

spelling in Kufic characters
the secrets, the signs
of marvellous calligraphy
that gave the game away
when love derives
from rules, from procedures,
from proper scores
as scores were settled
by their luck and skill.

The young men of Aleppo,
gathered to pray,
stared in breathless wonder
at the severed head
of John the Baptist, caught in a net,
the blood still dripping red,
lips still moving, speaking
in the pattern of honeycomb
sweetening the thirsty boys
playing by
the rules, the procedures,
the proper scores
as scores were settled
by their luck and skill.

Years later in Aleppo, these boys,
now aged, gathered to hear
the sentence passed on them
by virgins, by martyrs —
crème de la crème —
who listened, all ears,
to cries of despair
from the crowd of spectators
willing on the players
obeying all

the rules, the procedures,
the proper scores
as scores were settled
by their luck and skill.

Neptune

Un punto solo m'è maggior letargo
che venticinque secoli alla 'mpressa,
che fe' Nettuno ammirar l'ombra d'Argo
                    — Dante, *Paradiso, Canto 33,* lines 94-96

Neptune arrived from under the water
hitching a lift from Jason's Argonauts.
Adorning himself in a golden fleece,
he surveyed the marvelling multitudes.
He provided means for scuba divers
to play harmonies we no longer hear,
translating heaven into tongues of fire —
strangely melodious cantos of grief.
He blessed the damned and fed them the ocean,
drowning sorrows with pint Guinness bottles,
the best of gargle, magnificent brew
straight from the stills of the Tower of Babel.
Half-man, half-monster, half-dolphin, half-cod,
Neptune was more than the sum of his parts.

This god could ask forgiveness of his wife,
shaving her legs with a bolt of lightning.
She sold her skin for the shoes on her feet,
abandoning the sea for a softer life.
Robbed by her elders, craved by her betters,
a bull in a china shop raped her.
He pieced together the broken Dresden
of her features smashed beyond recognition.
They kissed, they made up, the wedding breakfast
consisted of orange and lemon silk.
Someone would have to pay for that piper.
Who hears such demands leagues beneath the sea?
He prided himself on having no manners.
He did a runner — left Earth to herself.

The Boys of Summer

The boys of summer
now have sons who play
at being boys.
The ships they sailed
were seven ships
from all the seven seas.

They broke the ice
but froze to death,
they starved and turned to stone,
till fathers warmed
the beds for them,
their frozen drunken sons.

It took an age
to get across
the message loud and clear.
They were the ghosts
who slept with ghosts
called father and called son.

American Football in Booterstown Park

After six months the grass grows again.
The Christmas ice rink very few wanted —
that's long dismantled and melted in rain.
Nobody weeps for its loss — we're well rid
of figures of eight the skaters circled,
taking deep breaths as if life depended
on staying erect. The freezing fires of hell
wait for those damned by what's been done and said.
Time to bury all that is bitter and dark:
the summer's come back to Booterstown Park.

Their fat loins girded, their elegant arse
bound tight as most delicate Chinese feet,
sharp to the touch like the yellowest gorse,
American footballers congregate.
They do not entirely understand the score
of the game they play against each other
engaging in what is uncivil war —
brother beating the crap out of brother.
They live for the logo they choose to wear.
Blood is thicker than mineral water.

June brings these migratory birds to us,
searching for diamonds in the Bird Sanctuary.
A sign of intelligent life, a cause —
just to believe in the land of the free.
I wait an age for the Number 7,
rattling the fare in my jeans pocket.
I could throw money — pennies from heaven —
to bless the boys in their ludicrous kit.
They have eyes only for the task in hand.
To win, to touch down — that I understand.

I hear the medley of each dialect
from the four corners of this island
at the Sunday game, risking their neck
to score for the parish across the ocean.
More power to their arm, their fist, the caul
at the top of their most breakable scalp —
they watch the birdie, they rise and they fall,
they give the bastards opposite a skelp.
They pray for rain to drench the playing fields:
they look to the earth for a better yield.

They have the luck to be clean as whistles,
and nothing is stained by the blood of slaves.
Let us salute them as knights of the realm,
domain of the paleskin, home of the brave.
Their holdalls contain the robes of saffron,
Argyll socks, winklepickers, kipper ties —
strange uniforms of a lost dimension
where nobody ever has to say goodbye.
The sea disgorged these dolphins and sharks:
American Football in Booterstown Park.

Claudia

in memory of Claudia Victoria, daughter of Claudia Severne, died age 10 years, 1 month and 11 days, circa 3rd century AD, Lyons

A panther came to visit me.
He carried the god Bacchus.
I fed the panther rabbit,
a piece of beef,
a shank of lamb.
It was never enough.
The panther still was hungry.
It asked for more and more,
it needed human flesh.
I prayed to great god Bacchus,
save me from your panther.
He drinks me like darkness.
The garlands in my brother's hair,
they turn to stone.
My mother's face is winter.
Counting my years, my months, my days,
she takes my last breath.
I try to grasp my mother's hands.
She did her best to save me.

Tomato's Gay Bar in Tokyo

You will not find
the likes of Percy French
being roared to the rafters
nor a man called Michael
or Thomas among the denizens
of salary men who gather
after hunting the yen
in Tomato's karaoke bar
where kiss and tell
is not the rage in Tokyo —

don't mention the war
but look at snapshots
of wives and children
whose pride and joy are
on the bullet train
from this to the next world
connecting Nagasaki
to railways in Clare
vanishing through limestone —
a kamikaze rose.

Isaac Newton Falls in Love

His body tastes the same as pears,
I buy him oranges and apples.

Celestial, his mouth a star,
I see him, and the sun, it pales.

Creature

I know a creature that cannot be known.
I fell in love with his flesh and forelock,
head over heels with that beast and his like —
let him devour me out of house and home.
Beautiful creature, my sore heart's desire,
he took a bite out of my nothingness:
the pain was a place where I could find rest,
spaced out on the straw of his underwear.
Smelling a rat pissing on chaff and corn,
I settle scores with his ghost for the night
he upped from our bed to hit the town,
wishing to Christ he had never been born,
scorning the splendid and roseate light
virgins unravelled for their wedding gown.

The Blue Envelope

after Charlie Brady

I opened the blue envelope.
In there, what would I find?
The Atacama Desert;
a lottery ticket;
that broken wedding ring —
the one you remember.
One you must remember.

It got lost in the garden.
Would it ever be found?
The orchard shed blossoms.
Apples soured on the branches.
Who said open the blue envelope?
There it was — the wedding ring;
the Atacama Desert.

The Old House

I saw a stranger
sitting in shirt sleeves
outside our old house,
38 Marian Park.
I didn't know him,
nor did he know me
as he sits, as I pass by,
trying not to look.

Will he wander inside,
remarking to his wife,
who do we know
with greying red hair?
He was eyeing the house,
not too suspicious,
but we should be careful
when we lock up at night.

And my father's ghost,
my mother's ghost,
they give me a key,
welcoming me home,
saying, break in,
scare the life out of him,
the living daylights
inside the old house.

Stalingrad

Ice sticks in my throat like a herring's bones.
I long for salt, a Jewish bride, to bless
the bread and smash the glass opaquely clear
as ice.
      Our army — a headless statue
carried for luck through Stalingrad to lift
the plague and curse the priests brought to their knees —
could do no more than wave rifles above
the doors, the window frames, the slates of roofs
where we sought shelter from the war, eating
flesh, warm as flesh, of guns in Stalingrad.

Westmeath

in memory of Josephine Hart

The fields of Westmeath,
the wilds of Westmeath.

Water
in that part of the world
purifies itself
in beads of sorrow.
Those same fields
yield a strange crop —
wheat that turns bread
back into wheat,
tasting of salt,
of ovens in your mouth.
Home
in that part of the world
was a place to leave behind,
searching for something to frighten me.
Imagine the surprise
when I found it
in the purity of water,
of salt,
the sorrow of bread and wheat,
the same crop
of those strange fields —

the fields of Westmeath,
the wilds of Westmeath.

Boyfriends

The men I loved have aged well.
Some even married lookers.
Their women gave birth to sons
who resembled their mothers.

These men no longer call,
no knocking at my door —
no longer look for sustenance,
my shadow's wings and more.

Lost boys, they had their uses,
those men who always married —
said their say, paid their way
and then did their harm.

Still I should forgive them
since what will be will be —
boyfriends giving life to sons,
boyfriends, who once loved me.

The Peace Process

for Paddy and Penny Sleeman

The merlin smelt
a dirty rat
in a shape
not his brother.

The sky's a pit
set for fights —
white feather, scarface,
knuckleduster.

The thrush, it bares
a mighty fist —
all's up for grabs,
the whole Kabbalah.

Chanting psalms,
they square the circle —
praise the Lord's
soft ammunition.

Hungry for home,
they might consume
the brown, the pink,
the chaffinch wing.

It flies to freedom
pacifying
the tender, mad,
the merlin, thrush.

PART FOUR

Cherry Blossom

for Rebecca Pelan

The cherry blossom
by the Science building
comes from Japan.
It feeds on rice
from the north wind.
It shuns the rose.

Beautiful men in dress suits
knotting their bow ties
smell of the moon's
essence most sweet,
they swear to be true
by these blooms.

Healthy as sin,
they are the tree of knowledge
in the genesis
of my garden
I did loot and pillage —
none could resist.

Except the rain.
It kissed the blossoms,
and they thrived.
Who would believe
the miracle no saint
nor scholar shamed?

The lake by the Science building
is full of flowers.
They discard their clothing,
unknot their bow ties.

They swim in placid water,
they touch each other's eyes.

Light
from the cherry blossoms
illuminates the night.
Daughters of the universe,
all blood and nerves,
bless each mother's son.

The Freeman's Journal

What can I read in the *Freeman's Journal*?
The earthquake in Lisbon did not happen.
A mad cow was slaughtered in County Louth.
Two dancing bears were incarcerated.

Guess what I read in the *Freeman's Journal*?
A woman gave birth to a tsetse fly.
Blood is made up of tomato ketchup.
The proof God exists is the human eye.

Tsetse flies swarm above slaughtered cattle.
Convoys are taking coffins to Lisbon.
There are bears prowling streets in County Louth.
Cover their traces in the *Freeman's Journal*.

The Russian Ship in the Swilly

The feast of St Blaise
we exposed our bare throats
to the holy smelling oil
carried all the way to Fahan
from four corners of the globe
on the Russian ship
anchored in Lough Swilly
to dredge for herrings,
mackerel and dead souls —
tangled treasure in their nets
they hauled to the round sky
like silver stars on their steeple,
dismantling the blue face,
the steadfast, surly lip
of St Mura's Cross,
weathered into nothingness,
a fine featureless stone,
Cyrillic, mystical,
Braille for the seeing eye
ready for the war to end wars
waged by sheets of rain,
the wind, the voices unceasing
warning Ludden and Tooban
about the Russian ship
coming to transport us all —
each man jack, woman and child —
to Odessa and to Kiev,
the port of Archangel,
where it is we will belong.

Music

This year I stopped listening to music.
When I say stopped listening, I mean stopped.
Radios in taxis, din on a bus,
restaurants playing waiters' favourites,
their bow ties the blue of the marks I'd leave
on every art and part of their bodies
taking too long to serve expensive food
that tastes like music I refuse to hear.
Why does it now turn my entire stomach?
Why can I no longer listen to music?

I can still hear angels rip rooms to shreds.
All you need do is call them, they will come
like dogs of war, herring bones down their throat,
a voice draining the cup of home, home
where the heart stopped, the music stopped beating.
What I could hear, never now forgotten,
was occurring in the pardon of seas,
a holy family blessing itself,
throwing water into nooks and crannies
of rooms angels tore, as I say, to shreds.

They searched for hell, they searched for heaven,
hell and heaven one and the same abode
to those who stopped listening to music,
radios in taxis, din on a bus,
wondering when was it that this happened?
When did it cease healing, cease giving hope,
music like a bow tie and boys' blue eyes
taking their time to survey the whole joint,
saying nothing, singing nothing, obliged
to no one, free and happy, like music?

Margaret Barry

She churns her butter from the sun's milk in the whin bush.

She beats the eggs of eagles doused in the best of strong porter.

Down the hatch in one heave and let rip like flames from
    paraffin
a song the rainbow taught her one night she tamed it for her
    beast of burden
to carry her if she so chose to hell or Connaught, depending
    on her mood.

Those same moods have been known to swell Atlantic waves
    and crack rocks
as if they were soft caramels in her mouth panting for some-
    thing stronger.

A man would do, but failing that, a god with limbs of gold
    — he would suffice.

One Easter Day she woke the dead lamenting for the life of
    her father and mother.
They chided her, saying, Margaret, you have the voice of an
    angel, daughter,
a ministering angel — that should be your consolation, girl.

She took them at their word and raised her lips heavenwards.
What came from her mouth was music could comfort lonely
    Lucifer.

She stilled the cosmos, and the sun was heard in fits of laughing.
Margaret Barry was the woman pitied his fire and mopped his
    brow.
He took her in his arms and played her sweet as a French
    melodeon.

He thought her his, so hadn't he the neck to fall asleep on
   herself.
In his dreams he saw her crowned Queen of Spain, and all
   its dominions.
She sailed off with all his treasures of the Sierra Madre.

From that day on there was no want of whin, eagles or porter.

The Stillorgan Road

Years ago a girl took flight,
imagining her skylark wings,
into the mountainous air
above the Stillorgan Road.
Or did she glimpse a hummingbird,
flamboyant plumage of the male,
alien to Donnybrook,
seeking passage to go home?

Cars beneath the Belfield bridge,
they sway like silver birch in winds
that purify the hard of heart
along the Stillorgan Road.
Athletes race and chase the time —
faster, fast, a second off.
They do not nod; they do not wave;
they know the direction home.

It may be they've been here before,
transmigrant souls just passing through —
halting site for next to nothing
beside the Stillorgan Road.
The week's wages I would spend
to raise the dead and stir the blood
tasting of wine from hummingbirds,
their plumage and the skylark's bones.

Tewkesbury Abbey

Last summer it was flooded.

Father, mother, uncles in tow,
they arrive with three children.
Tewkesbury Abbey welcomes
no one — a wedding is planned
for invited guests only.
And so they eat lunch together.

Last summer it was flooded.

They drink the rain of orange juice,
eat clay of chicken sandwich,
feast on a swarm of locusts,
the jawbone of sour honey —
the clouds on this horizon,
they shadow Tewkesbury Abbey.

Last summer it was flooded.

The clergy bolt the doors
dissolving Tewkesbury Abbey.
It reopens at four.
We drive in separate cars
back to our destination —
the house that is not theirs.

Last summer it was flooded.

The Travels of Marco Polo

Limerick Junction and Marco Polo —
he's seen boarding the train from Charleville.
The silk road goes all the way to Mallow.
Expect a great feed of mulberry leaves.
Dodging the fare, wise to every scam,
he was happy enough to travel blind,
this high-born Venetian gentleman.

A chargeable animal, humankind —
after a dose of the roughest poitín,
falling downstairs and cursing to heaven,
feeding on calf with the prodigal son,
sharing a name with old father Adam,
he knelt in the family pagoda,
fat as the Buddha, dreaming of China.

The Belly of the Whale

Last night I went searching
for what's not easy found —
a good man in this country
where all are duty bound
to steal what you most cherish,
spit on your good name,
mock a man's misfortunes,
delight in his shame.

Last night I went travelling
without ship or sail,
last night I went fishing
in the belly of the whale.
I caught jewels and diamonds,
fish to beat the band.
I held God almighty
in the palm of my hand.

Can I take you travelling
without ship or sail?
Will you come out fishing
in the belly of the whale?
I know what you're thinking,
a good man's hard to find.
In this darkest country
I can read your mind.

Mock a man's misfortunes,
delight in his shame,
steal what he'll most cherish,
spit on his good name —
we caught jewels and diamonds,
fish to beat the band,
we held God almighty
in the palm of our hand.

Kennedy in Ireland

1

The first man we saw with skin tanned,
stopping to shake the good nuns' hands,
finding time always for the holy sisters.
In his face we could read fear of Cuba,
in his voice strains of the boys of Wexford.
Clap hands for daddy, daddy coming home,
sweeties in his pocket, coming cross the sea,
to save us one and all — did we need saving?
Did we need sweeties?
                              Kennedy in Ireland.

2

We drank him like water from a spring well.
We fetched him his tea in fine bone china.
We fed him soft eggs poached in pure silver.
Full Irish breakfast, sausage and bacon,
came from animals cured in Atlantis.
Salmon smoked itself to perfection.
Tongues spoke in Cajun, a wondrous French
with a trace of the *blás* best detected
east of the Shannon.
                              Kennedy in Ireland.

3

To guard against polio, swallow up
a sugar cube stained archangel yellow.
Shirtless in singlets, we were all lined up,
the boys who'd be facing the firing squad.
Myself being first to take weak and faint,

stinging like nettles, stilling the playground,
I could hear teachers whisper to teachers,
something's amiss, seriously amiss —
as if they could break, fifty years onward,
the power of the spell leaving men gasping
for life, for breath, clapping hands for daddy,
daddy coming home, crossing the ocean,
sweeties in his pocket.
                              Kennedy in Ireland.

The Guest House

for Jean

This is a warm house. Warm as the welcome.
The fans cool the beautiful salmon. It is pink.
So are the potatoes. Skin tastes of kind earth.

The water in the pool is kind. It is blue.
This is a house whose colours are the globe.
A painting of three sisters imagines one absent.

This is the guest house. The welcome is warm.
Here's where they serve cold beer in coloured bottles.
They are brown, and the wine is fierce as red.

It is good wine. And it is excellent beer.
Make yourself at ease in that big leather chair.
Should you sit there and suffer from the heat —

let there be no suffering in this warm house.
The gentle deer come and pester this parched lawn.
I would invite them, but they don't eat salmon.

They don't drink wine. When they sleep they forget.
I like remembering. I like the colours of the globe,
houses where the fans cool the beautiful beer.

This is the guest house. The welcome is fierce.

The Fire Alarm

It could happen — remember that.
The kaddish of the siren's keen
down the circle of corridors
empties the rooms of kith and kin.
To use the lift is dangerous.
We wait with patience on the street
holding cups of lukewarm coffee
sweetened by dreams of missed meetings.
My socks are blue, my shoes polished,
my neck well scrubbed, my mind mislaid.
Boys next door in each other's arms
press the flesh of pleasant fire.

The German Embassy in Trimleston

We never heard
the Valkyrie singing
as they gave birth
to beautiful Uzis —
a thousand virgins
all called Ursula
coming to Köln
to choose their own goddess.

I cannot tell you
who it is she might be —
far from the war
of ideas we live,
far from Ulrike Meinhof
we were reared,
taking machetes
to cut the state's throat,
slit body and soul,
dismember the Volk.

That's how I think
walking through Trimleston,
queues of all kinds
at the Embassy gates,
a patient gang
dreaming of Germany,
fearing no guards
in the unmanned sentry —
no smell of guns
nor bombs laced with petrol
spilling their rainbows
on the streets of Derry,
chewing our fingernails
down to the quick.

On my way to work
past the dry cleaners
I wonder why it moved,
the German Embassy,
lock, stock and barrel,
safe to this suburb
of fantastic beasts
who roam through our campus
baring their fangs,
deranging the young,
asleep, crying wolf
to Ulrike Meinhof
who opens her throat
and howls at the moon.

For reasons unknown
to master and maid —
or if they know why
then they're not saying —
when did they up camp
to live in our midst,
happy ever after?

Are they happy, you think,
in Trimleston Avenue,
ensconced in concrete,
the German Embassy,
yearning for mother
and for fatherland,
eating lamb and couscous
now that the war's over?
Yes, the war is over.

The Monkey Puzzle

in memory of Nóirín Moynihan

If I could wish you strength
it would be to climb the trees of Eden,
trees of knowledge, trees of light.
When you reach the top,
the top of the trees of light,
I would feed you knowledge
sweet and sour as apples,
knowledge you would not forbid,
apples to bite into.

Your hand, it is always hungry,
it is always open.
I would press into your hand,
your hand that is always closing,
fruit, and you would devour it —
healing alien, a handsome devil
who came all the way from Asia
making you remember you asked —
you asked remember me.

Remember the spoils of war,
battles, truce and drums
that pelt from Africa,
the pipes, the pipes that call
from the banks of Slaney,
river banks that echo
the caw of swans, thrush, wren and dove,
ravens bringing their young
to feast in Eden.

Trees of forbidden fruit
are monkey puzzles
across the road from the church.

The road is leading to Asia,
to Africa, to Eden.
If I could wish you strength
it would be to question
is there such a thing
as spoils of war,
as trees saying Mass,
the trees of Eden,
the monkey puzzle.

Ariadne

I am a woman without a shadow.
I weave the sun from my mother's sore tears.

I wear her warnings like a brown birthmark —
my fair sister stole my husband from me.

I watched his love turn from gold to rust.
He placed that ring on my broken finger.

My heart was Minoan alabaster
that pair of fuckers — Theseus, Phaedra —

spat on, danced on, smashed into nothing,
squealing like bulls on the way to slaughter.

Or was it pigs beneath the farmer's knife,
salting the meat of their dirty story?

Fit for the byre, two beasts in the bedroom.
My wedding gift was a dowry of poison.

Cheers to the pair who deserve each other.
Their children bled in baths of red water.

I wash their hair with their mother's salt tears.
I am the sun that casts only shadows.

The Governess Grave in Mount Jerome

In Mount Jerome
there is a grave —
there is a grave
in Mount Jerome.

A hundred thousand
million of souls
turned to diamond
in the dull clay.

Their bags snatched,
their balls kicked,
they'd take the feet
from under you.

They hear the name
of governess —
it slaps them sharp
across the cheek.

And spectacles
are sent flying.
Bird women,
they go berserk.

Lost in their dreams,
half starved of sleep,
they wear their rings
through the nose.

My bearded ladies
shaved their legs
to marry well,
then froze to death —

Antarctica.
Cold water washed
the women's shrouds.
They still were soiled.

There is a grave
in Mount Jerome —
in Mount Jerome
there is a grave.

Carnivores on Iona

Were I you I'd settle for dragon pie,
the beast of burden St Columba rode,
his beehive cell carried on his sore back,
never again setting sight on Ireland.
Scholarly sinners thriving on burgers,
bottles of lager, uppers and downers,
we who were carnivores on Iona
discover where there be fathers, mothers,
breathing out fire, swimming to the mainland,
demanding more drinks, more drinks for ladies —
optics of Scotch, fiascos of wine,
rejecting the medium rare roast lamb.
Were I you I'd settle for dragon pie.

The Montrose Hotel

for Declan and Beth

They say a flock of swans
nested in the Montrose Hotel.
Christ, were they obstinate creatures,
refusing to be ousted.

They fouled the sheets and blankets.
They stained every carpet.
Their wings white umbrellas,
they brought the rain with them.

They say some kind of plague
settled in the Montrose Hotel.
We've never known the like,
nor would you want to know it.

The swans themselves could not care less
of the panic they had caused,
content to squander seeds
of the most luscious corn.

They bake themselves sweet bread
in the hotel's burning oven.
They warm their webbed feet
in the declining sun.

The swans invite the homeless
to share their winter feast,
providing bed and breakfast
for what is next to nothing.

A swarm of bees accompany
the destitute and poor,

looking to find pollen
in a vase of withered flowers.

They say it's a rough business,
managing a hotel.
They say the times are crazy —
a plague of bees and swans.

In a Town of Five Thousand People

In a town of five thousand people
those who've never wept nor torn their hair
from the roots will be found living near water.

In a town of five thousand people
men downing too much drink dreaming
of wives who died walk out halfway through Mass.

In a town of five thousand people
there are boys kicking the lining out of boys
whose mothers watch through windows.

In a town of five thousand people
the same windows hear mothers weeping,
tearing hair from roots, downing too much dreams.

In a town of five thousand people
they worship the goat, they sacrifice rams,
they drink bull's blood August bank holiday.

In a town of five thousand people
the dumb and the deaf, the lame and blind
speak and sing, they see and dance near water.

In a town of five thousand people
the fathers are deaf, the mothers blind,
children in windows weep mother, father.

In a town of five thousand people
trees in the red of orchards know better than most
there's no such thing as forgiveness.

In a town of five thousand people
thieves in the night steal apples and brew
Babycham and brandy in the back yard.

In a town of five thousand people
the brandied Babychams go to the head —
who knows if what happened has happened?

In a town of five thousand people
sorrow takes the shape of the steeple
in the faith of once upon a time.

In a town of five thousand people
fathers, mothers wept for mothers, fathers
remembering once upon a time.

In a town of five thousand people
the goats and rams drank blood in the night
as they worshipped and sacrificed orchards.

In a town of five thousand people
mothers and fathers, orchards and apples,
are kicking the lining out of goats and rams.

In a town of five thousand people
I am certain all will be forgiven,
downing too much dreams, tearing hair from roots.

In a town of five thousand people
where mothers and fathers are weeping
I'll do a runner and leave well alone.

In a town of five thousand people
five thousand sisters, five thousand brothers
raise their voice, egging me to return.

In a town of five thousand people
I will argue morphine should be given
to those who can hear windows weeping.

In a town of five thousand people
the morphine will turn me into an orchard —
into mother, father, hair from the roots.

In a town of five thousand people
I will be goat, I will be ram dreaming,
I will be found grazing near water.

In a town of five thousand people
from the faith of once upon a time
I'll do a runner and leave well alone.

In a town of five thousand people
in a town of five thousand people
in a town of five thousand people.